Virginia's Nuggets of Life

A Helper's Heart

ISBN: 978-1-7337342-6-4 (Paperback)

First printing, 2020

Shameka Howell
P.O. Box 322
Jackson, GA 30233

Shamekah2@gmail.com

Foreword
By Shameka Howell

This book is a lasting tribute to how good my grandmother is to people and how great she has been over the years. I owe who I am, to my grandmother and I tribute my being to her. She is where I came from. I am standing on my grandmother's shoulders.

This book helps us to see why our family is the way it is.

Who encouraged you, who looked out for you, why are you the way that you are today? I honor my grandmother for her cultivating me into who I am today. I wanted something that I could pass on to my kids and my grandkids so they could say that my great grandmother made a lasting impact. I think that it is important that we store those memories and share them with our loved ones. This book is going to bless the Humphrey family.

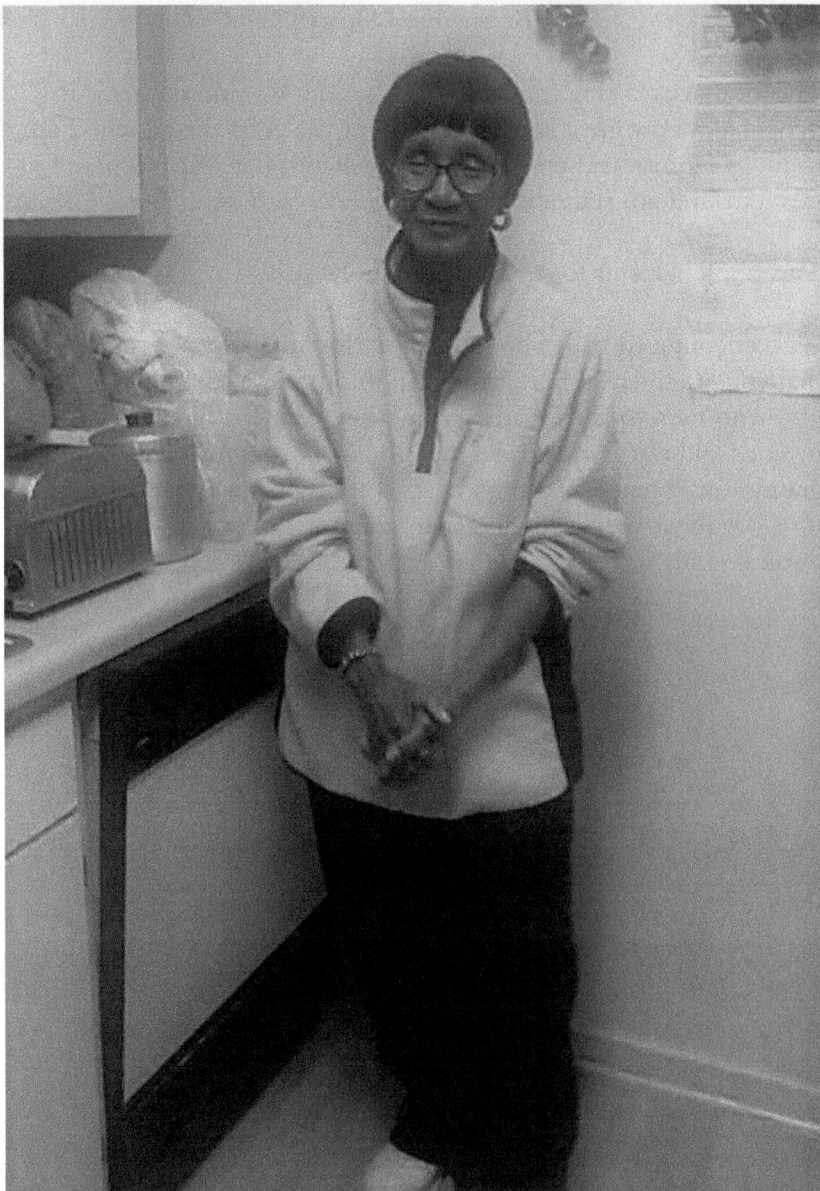

Table of Contents

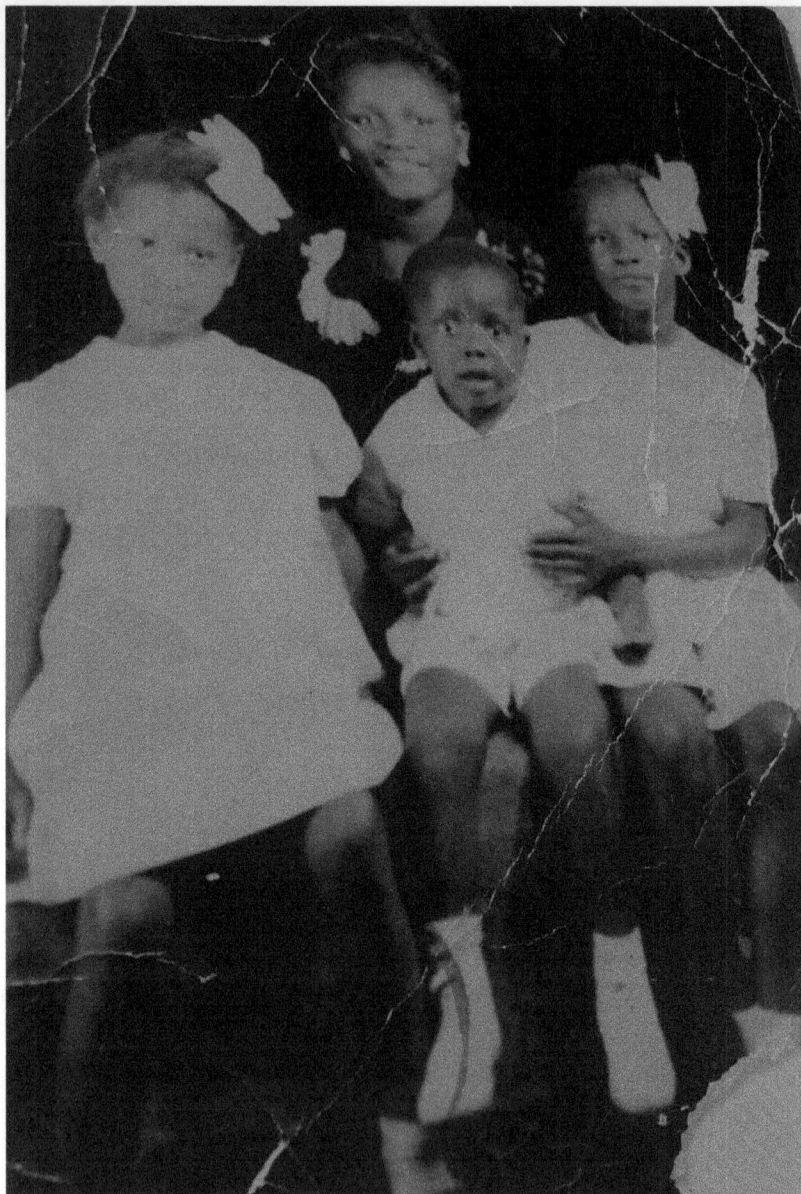

~ My Aunt and Father's Love

- **What has been instilled in you by your loved ones that has helped form you into who you are today?**

My mother died when I was about 12. I had a sister named Annette (who is deceased now) and brother named George who is still living. No one wanted all 3 children when my mother passed. They wanted to split us up. People were willing to take one child a piece, but not all 3. My aunt Ida did not have any children, so she gave up her life to raise us. She opened her doors to all 3 of us and took us in like her own. My aunt Ida was a very smart woman who always put God first. She owned houses and cars and was very successful. She was self-sufficient, and she provide for all 3 of us, over and beyond what we would have ever expected. My aunt taught me about being independent, being clean, and to always share regardless of what you had.

Aunt Ida gave us everything. We did not want for anything. We always had houses and cars and everything that we needed.

My aunt had four houses when she died. She was successful and had all of her affairs in order. When she died, she had left us a good amount of money. I was so shocked because I had never seen that much money in my life.

My aunt Ida did not have any pride. She helped everyone and never complained. No one knew how much my aunt had helped so many people.

I think that I take after my aunt Ida in a lot of ways. I love helping people and I do not publicize when I do. So many people call me mama. So many young men on drugs and they respect me as Mama in their life. I pray for them and I believe that God hears and answers my prayers.

My aunt and my daddy were a blessing to others because they were blessed.

~Booker

My father Booker was a street hustler who came in my life when I got older. I guess with him being so glad to finally be in my life, he would bless me with anything. One day he asked me was I saving for a rainy day. *He stressed that bad times are going to come so I should equip myself for the bad times.* And until this very day, when I am doing good, I buy extra stuff. I prepare for rainy days. I learned the value of saving from my father.

I remember one time I went to my father to ask for something. I was dating someone at the time. I told my father that I had a good man. My father just listened to me talk. After I finished bragging on my man, my daddy told me that I did not have to tell him that I had a good man. He told me that if I had a good man, it would show in the end. If I really had a good man, I would not be there asking him for help. *A woman with a good man would not be in lack.*

My dad taught me that when I have extra money, to buy two things at a time. Being able to store up for a rainy day, has really helped me navigate life in amazing ways. I have not dealt with lack because of the principles that my father taught me.

My aunt and father had so much wisdom. My aunt and my daddy were a blessing to others because they were blessed.

Everything that I learned was through God, my aunt, and my father.

~ *Introduction to God*

- **How has God touched you and let you know that He is real?**

My grandma took me to church and every time I got to church; I would shout. I just could not help it. I would get so overwhelmed with emotion and joy that I just had to shout and get it out. I could just feel that God was there, and He was so good. I could not contain my praise. It's been in me since I was about 8 years old. My grandma used to say "Bunky (my nickname) don't shout when you get in this church" and I would tell her "Ok grandma". When I would get in church, I could not help myself, I would shout. *I was just so happy, and I just loved helping people*. I thank God for guidance from my God-fearing family. My grandmother and aunt were instrumental in introducing me to God.

God whoops me when I try to fake with Him.

I remember when I was at a low place spiritually and tried to kill myself by taking aspirin. I told God that I can't take no more and that I was tired. I was ready to end my life. I swallowed the aspirin thinking that I was going to end my life. *Lo and behold, the aspirin stayed in my throat for a week*. God would not let the aspirin go down my throat. I was so sick, and the aspirin just wouldn't go down. It just sat in the back of my throat. After that I never tried to kill myself again. To this day, I won't even look at an aspirin bottle.

One day when I was young, I cursed everyone out. Everyone that I passed in the street, I just cursed at them. My aunt Ida called me in the house and asked me was I being bad. I told my aunt that I wasn't doing anything wrong. That night while I was sleeping, I woke up and saw my deceased mother. I was so scared. My mother was sitting there with a white dress on and a white flower in her head. I had previously prayed to God to never let me see my mother deceased. That night when I saw her, I was scared straight. After that night, my aunt didn't have any more problems out of me. I instantly became the perfect child.

I accepted Christ as my personal Lord and Savior when I was close to 8 years old. There was a blind lady named Ms. Eula Mae who lived on my street. When I would help her, she would sing to me and I just loved it. I was always running up and down the street helping people. I would just go from house to house and see who needed help with something. I found great joy and satisfaction in being able to help people. I really felt like God was using me. At 8 years old, I felt like an extension of God's hands.

I did have a brother. My brother was sentenced to die via the electric chair. I went to see him every Saturday and I prayed for him. I do not remember how it all happened, but to this day he is saved, off of death row and out of prison. He is also married to the woman that stood by him through everything he went through. Once again, God allowed me to see my prayers for my brother answered.

I remember when I had surgery, the doctor that performed it was a very special person. There was something about his stature that provided me with such a sense of peace when he came to talk to me before the surgery. My healing was so supernatural. God really showed His hand throughout that process. So now when I am feeling low, I reflect on my surgeon. His spirit. As believers we need other people to help us on this journey besides our pastors! We need pastors, but we also need other people who can minister to us when we go through rough times.

God wants us to show that we are blessed. God wants us to represent Him well... to take pride in our appearance.

I rely on the book of Psalm especially when I am going through rough times. My favorite scripture in the Bible is

Psalm 23 (King James Version)
[1] The Lord is my shepherd; I shall not want.

[2] He maketh me to lie down in green pastures: he leadeth me beside the still waters.

[3] He restoreth my soul: he leadeth me in the paths of righteousness for his name's sake.

[4] Yea, though I walk through the valley of the shadow of death, I will fear no evil: for thou art with me; thy rod and thy staff they comfort me.

[5] Thou preparest a table before me in the presence of mine enemies: thou anointest my head with oil; my cup runneth over.

[6] Surely goodness and mercy shall follow me all the days of my life: and I will dwell in the house of the Lord forever.

A few of the scriptures that have helped me in my lowest times are:

Psalm 35 (KJV)
[1] Plead my cause, O Lord, with them that strive with me: fight against them that fight against me.

[6] Let their way be dark and slippery: and let the angel of the Lord persecute them.

[28] And my tongue shall speak of thy righteousness and of thy praise all the day long.

Psalm 37 (KJV)
Fret not thyself because of evildoers, neither be thou envious against the workers of iniquity.

[40] And the Lord shall help them and deliver them: he shall deliver them from the wicked, and save them, because they trust in him.

Psalm 91 (KJV)

[1] He that dwelleth in the secret place of the most High shall abide under the shadow of the Almighty.

[2] I will say of the Lord, He is my refuge and my fortress: my God; in him will I trust.

Psalm 121 (KJV)

[1] (A Song of degrees.) I will lift up mine eyes unto the hills, from whence cometh my help.

[2] My help cometh from the LORD, which made heaven and earth.

Each of these scriptures serves as reminders that no matter what or who comes against me, God will always defend me. He shows me through His word how much he loves and is concerned about me.

~ *Wisdom Comes from Obedience*

- **What has been the negative effects on your life from not obeying the still small voice of God?**

They saw in church that I didn't do gossip. Out of 40 years I have never been in my pastor's office for something negative. I just obey God. God is a spirit and He will speak. Things come to your spirit to tell you which way to go. If I did wrong; that would let me know that I did not comprehend what He said. When it comes back to my spirit it gives me an opportunity to get it right.

Just like the other day the Lord told me to go to the store and buy some food. I obeyed and by the time that I got back home, it had started to pour down raining. ***I don't have a car but I have an umbrella.*** I take the bus where I need to go. I realize that my God given assignment is on public transportation to witness to people. I have more reach by being surrounded by people than sitting inside a car. I choose to obey God and go where He say go and say what He says. It doesn't bother me not to have a car. I feel a sense of purpose when I am able to encourage as many people as I can come in contact with within a day. Just to be able to share with them the Good News that Jesus loves them, does me a world of good. I learned not to question God.

Obeying God gave me wisdom.

I love to do things for people. I don't look down on people. There's no color for me. Everyone is the same.

People need to know that they are loved. No matter what you go through in this world, God is with you.

In my church I have served in different auxiliaries. Each auxiliary taught me the meaning of God.

~ Giving God Glory
- **What is the Beauty for Ashes narrative in your life?**

Every day of my life I give God the praises first and then to my aunt Ida because she gave us a good life. My family was raised to fear God.

My Aunt Ida was instrumental in my relationship with God. I went to church every Sunday with her.

I'm 84 now and the most important part of my life was having a God-fearing aunt and family.

I desired to please the Lord and my Aunt Ida.

Although God took my mother, my aunt stepped in for me and I didn't want for anything. She had such a sharing heart.

I give God the praise because church fearing people kept me in church.

My aunt took me to church and inspired me on how to treat people.

I learned not to question God.

Obeying God gave me wisdom.

I love to do things for people. I don't look down on people. There's no color for me. Everyone is the same.

People know that they are loved.

No matter what you go through in this world, God is with you.

In my church I have served in different auxiliaries. Each auxiliary taught me the meaning of God.

~ *Grandchildren/Greatgrandchildren Are an Inheritance/ Shameka My Helper*

- **What will your legacy in the earth be?**

My greatest joy is my grand babies.

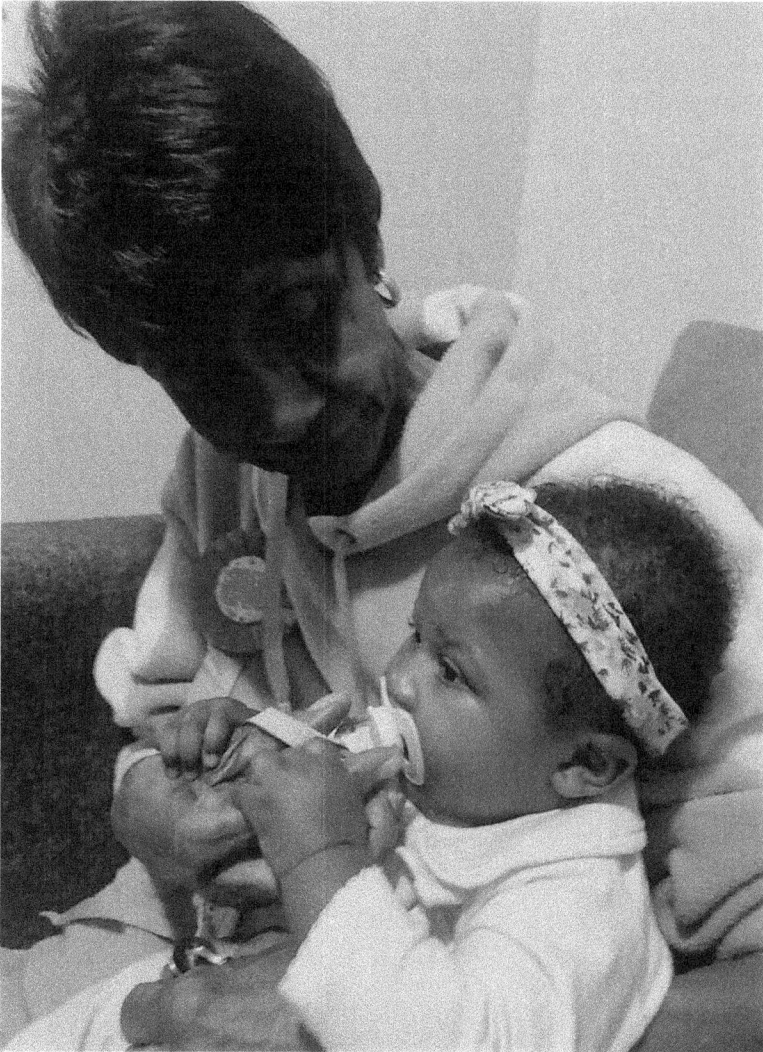

My granddaughter Shameka is an extraordinary person in the Lord.

Shameka is so unusual. She is so humble. I didn't have to want for anything. Shameka said grandma "I just love you so much". It would come from the Lord for her to do for me. Shameka has been an inspiration for me. She has helped me. Shameka is always helping someone. Shameka is just a beautiful person. If you are around her and walking with your head down, Shameka is going to do something for you. When I was going through my things Shameka was always there.

I love all my grandkids but Shameka and I have a very special relationship. It may be because when she went to college, I really took care of her so that she could focus on her schooling. Shameka has been such a blessing to me. I don't want for anything because Shameka always blesses me.
When you are doing God's work, God rewards you openly. Shameka and I have a special relationship and I really appreciate and love her.

When she told me that she wanted to do this I said Lord what do you want me to do because I like to stay in the background.

Shameka started helping me when she was in college. Shameka helps everyone. She does a lot for people and never wants to be recognized for her service. She is very humble. Shameka was a hard-working manager at a busy and famous shoe store. When she would see kids that didn't have shoes, she would buy them for them. Shameka would use her own money to buy shoes for kids that were struggling. Shameka is a good person and has been my inspiration. She is so low key, and she is a jewel. Shameka needs a book for young people to read about how she as young person has helped people know that God is real. Shameka never gives anyone any trouble. Shameka is a beautiful person. She is always helping people. I would love to see Shameka write a book because she deserves it. Shameka can bring people into God's Kingdom with her testimony. There are so many people going through that live around me. I ask God how I can reach them. Many young people are really lost and do not know that people love them, and that people care. Shameka should spread that joy for God and help the younger people.

The greatest joy of my life would be to look back and see the way God is rewarding Shameka for blessing so many people. Shameka should go around and let people know that they don't have to walk alone. Shameka's book would be beautiful, and it would give me the pleasure of my life. I know that Shameka has been good and humble and God loves humble people. I would be so happy to see Shameka write a book that lets people know that God is still real. It is bad out there now and I believe that Shameka can help them.

I love all of my grandchildren, but she is just an unusual gift.

I think God wanted me to grow by writing this book. God put Shameka around wisdom. She was always so humble and so appreciative.

When my mother died, no one wanted three children to raise. We went from house to house until my Aunt Ida took us all. Children will always have a special place in my heart. I have experienced hardship with having a child and trying to make ends meet. I can relate to all my children, grandchildren and great grandchildren. I love all of my children in a special way. They all look out for me in their own way and for that I'm grateful. I'm grateful to have lived to see a third generation of my family and to see everyone being successful at what they do best!

~ Endurance Anointing/ Helping Hand

- **What is your God given super power?**

At 84 years old the love of my aunt Ida, which was from the Lord made me more particular about doing it the right way.

I was always taught that the glory goes to God.

My greatest joy is to help somebody. You will never know that I have helped somebody because I never would publicize it. If I am giving someone a financial blessing, I would roll the money up in my hand and slide it in their hand discreetly. A person would never know that I just gave someone a blessing.

I believe that my dominant God characteristic is a Helping Hand. I get such joy when someone tells me that they love me. I know that I did something right. Not for me to get the glory but for God to get the glory.

I love children. I look at the way that we were raised, and God instilled in me to be there for children. To this day, continue to help raise my great grandchildren. I will forever be there for children. Being able to tend to children is actually a lifeline for me. They keep me active and engaged.

I worked at my job for 22 years and at my church for 40 years. I took care of 4 children and never missed a day of work. I kept my bosses house in order.

I started doing domestic work with Lisa and Stewart Butner. God has been so good to me and I get so full. They didn't know how to bless me when I retired, so they decided to send me a bonus every month to this day for being with them for 22 years.

If God takes me tomorrow, I can go to glory knowing that I have had a good life. My aunt raised me well, I have had houses, cars, and material things. I have never been in lack. God has just been blessing me.

~ Patience Is A Virtue

- **How has your plans for your life collided with God's plans for your life?**

Since I have been on my own, God has always had me around children. I thought that I would be working with patients doing healthcare, but God said that He was going to put me with children. My employer said that she never seen anyone like me. She said that she gets so frustrated with children and that I had so much patience with her children.

My shouting is my joy. Guys where I live at now call me mama. It's all about the way you approach people. People just need help. I was blessed to get the help that I needed, and I believe that it is my responsibility to bless others. If I be a blessing to you, be a blessing to someone else.

We should not judge people. If someone is drunk don't judge them. Put a dollar in their hand and tell them that God loves them. That should be your reasonable service.

~ *God' Supernatural Hand*

- **How has God exceeded your expectation in a scary situation?**

My obedience to God has allowed me to get to 84 yrs. old. I had surgery 2 years ago and God did something different for me.
My doctor explained the procedure to me, and God came through the doctor, and I felt no pain.
The doctor went through my navel for my surgery.
The Lord has done so many marvelous things for me. I try to live my life as an example.

God is doing so much for me that I am getting scared. God has blessed me so much. At 84 years old, I have only had one surgery and it was a beautiful surgery. No complications or anything. It's like I didn't even have surgery. He has just been so faithful and opening so many doors in my life. It's unbelievable at times how he just keeps on blessing me.

~ Final Nuggets

If you are sincere with God, He will see it.
That is my inspiration.
I try to stay humble because you do not know who you are going to meet.
If you do wrong, it will come back wrong.
If God take me today, don't cry for me because God has been so good to me. I really don't have any complaints. I just want to be Gods inspiration.

God has shown me not to give up.
A lot of guys call me Mama that are on drugs. I don't look at the drugs. If God tell me to tell them something, I do.

I am so overwhelmed with this book but if this is the way that God wants me to go, it will open up. I like being in the background and not being seen.

I would like to send a special thank you to all my children, grandchildren, and great grandchildren. Every one of them have been the driving force of my strength, faith and love.
My children Haroldine Benford, Anthony Humphrey, Sharon McDaniel (deceased), and Salafia Humphrey.
My grandchildren Shameka Howell, Ginica Humphrey, Maeisha Morales, Tiffany Humphrey, Joviera Humphrey, Deante Humphrey, and Stacy Grant (deceased). My great grandchildren Shebrekia Grant, Stacy Grant Jr. and Jameka Grant.
Great grandchildren Nathan and Torrey Howell Jr., Jeremiah Sturdivant, Jace and Jo'nae Kingsberry, Raymon Turner, Alexandria Humphrey, Parris Morales, Ethan Carson, Kenny Gibson, Jayden Cofield, Devonte Humphrey, Darius Tate Jr.

We want to say as the three of us Jamekia, Stacey and Shebrekia thank you for your infinite love and kindness, because every time we came down to Atlanta you always welcomed us with love and free arms. Grandma, you had the best cooking and you always made it with love and every time you cooked you always welcomed us to some. We always remembered there was times when dad used to call you 24/7, but no matter what you always showed love. Thank you for your amazing heart, knowledge, encouragement, joy, love and hugs and kisses. We love you and appreciate every moment we have spent with you.

- Love Jamekia, Stacey and Shebrekia

www.ingramcontent.com/pod-product-compliance
Lightning Source LLC
Chambersburg PA
CBHW060623070426

42449CB00042B/2483